A Client's Guide to Limited Legal Services

A Client's Guide to Limited Legal Services

M. SUE TALIA

Nexus Publishing Company
2333 San Ramon Valley Blvd., Suite 150
San Ramon, CA 94583-1613
510-838-2660

For more information, please contact Nexus Publishing Company,
2333 San Ramon Valley Boulevard, Suite 150,
San Ramon, California, 94583-1613.

First printing 1997.

ISBN 0-9651075-1-5

LCCN 97-67721

Cover and interior design by Allen M. Crider

Photograph by The Image Maker

Printed by Malloy Lithographing, Inc.

To all the caring family lawyers across the country who, despite the lack of support from their own bar associations, legislatures and courts, are courageously exploring new and innovative approaches to divorce in order to reduce the pain and conflict of families. In so doing, they are laying the groundwork for a new legal order.

Contents

Foreword

A new phenomenon is changing the face of family law and altering forever the way people approach their divorces. More specifically, it is altering the manner in which legal services are provided in divorce. Under the old paradigm, each party to a divorce hired a lawyer to handle all aspects of the case, giving the lawyer full responsibility and power over strategy and tactics. That practice is phasing out in some areas. In its place clients are demanding, and lawyers are offering, limited legal services. This means that a lawyer is retained only for specific tasks or limited substantive issues, or even as a "coach" doing little more than showing the client how to represent himself.

The reasons for these changes are complex. First and foremost, the court system is breaking down. As presently configured, the courts are simply unequipped to handle the deluge of divorce cases and family matters presented to them. Simultaneously, individuals are demanding greater control over their own life choices. This includes not only taking control back from lawyers, but even from the courts themselves. Much is written about the so-called "*pro per* crisis" in California and in other states, where phenomenally high numbers of family law litigants choose to represent themselves in family court. Sometimes as many as 75 percent of the cases have at least one side in *pro per*[1]. Frequently these choices result solely from financial necessity. However, in

---

[1] The terms *pro per* and *pro se* are used interchangeably in this guide. They mean a litigant who represents himself in court.

more and more cases, people who can afford lawyers insist on doing it themselves.

This is entirely new ground for both lawyers and litigants, and they are feeling their way as they redefine the traditional attorney-client relationship. In some states, the situation is complicated by the fact that it is being done under the disapproving eye of the state bar association; in others, it has official endorsement.[2]

This guide is intended to be a simple and practical handbook to educate family law litigants on limited legal services. In that way, you can make better decisions about entering into an agreement for legal services and defining its parameters. It contains sections on how to determine whether you are a good candidate for limited legal services, as well as detailed suggestions on how to structure the relationship. Most importantly, there are several appendices with checklists and questionnaires to help you evaluate your own case and abilities. Take the time to complete these fully and *in writing*, as they are the key to making good decisions about limiting legal services. You will find them most helpful if you complete them after reviewing the text.

No one wants to be forced to obtain and pay for services they don't want, simply because some regulatory agency insists upon it. What follows is designed to help you make the best possible decision while alerting you to common pitfalls.

I am going to be among the first to say that the family law system does not work. It is beyond the scope of this book to explain all of the reasons why. Unsatisfactory as it is, however, it is all we have right now. As long as a divorce isn't valid without a piece of paper signed by a judge, we will have to deal with the system in some way. This guide is designed to help you obtain that piece of paper with as little red tape and expense as possible while we all wait for something better to be devised.

If you are among those family law litigants who insist on having greater control over the process, increasing the scope of your

---

[2]Oregon is a notable example, as is the experiment in Maricopa County, Arizona.

own involvement and limiting that of your lawyer, God bless. You will find some useful suggestions in the pages which follow. Remember, however, that taking responsibility means precisely that: *Taking responsibility*. Be sure that you are qualified to perform the tasks you undertake, and then do so. If *you* want to be the one who makes the decisions about your divorce, you must be prepared to live with the consequences of those decisions, even if they turn out differently than you hoped or expected.

Many pioneering lawyers are willing to offer limited legal services to help you handle some or all aspects of your own divorce. They do it because they believe it is right and that the system is unduly complicated. Does this mean that even with an excellent "coach" you are going to know as much about family law as your lawyer does? Of course not. However, if you are willing to educate yourself on the law and the procedures as they apply to your case, and make careful decisions about how much of the legal work you can do yourself and what should be delegated to a specialist, you may be happier with the outcome than with the traditional approach. It does not, however, guarantee that you are going to get everything you want, any more than you would have under the old system.

Therefore, be honest with yourself and your lawyer about your abilities and instructions, educate yourself where necessary, and delegate to your attorney those tasks or issues which you are not qualified to handle. The point is to work as a team with your attorney to obtain the best possible result.

Good luck.

1

What is All This About Anyway?

Why Family Law?

It is no coincidence that family law litigation is at the cutting edge of the movement to limit legal services.

First, the very universality of the divorce experience means that a large percentage of our population is going to be thrust into the system at some time in their lives. The forms and procedures are frequently complex, and many people simply can't afford to pay someone else to represent them.

Moreover, in most states family law is *theoretically* set up so that individual litigants can represent themselves. Criminal law does not assume that the criminals are *pro se* (that is, self-representing). The criminal rules are very technical and everyone expects that with public defenders available, all accused criminals will have the benefit of competent legal counsel.

Not so, family law. Though the rules and procedures are hardly less technical than in criminal courts, there are few, if any, public agencies to step in and provide free legal services to family law litigants. Whatever funding is available for low-cost legal services in other fields usually dries up for family law. Frankly, the demand would be almost insatiable, and the money just isn't there.

Most legislatures like to tell themselves that they are "simplifying" procedures when they tinker with the family law forms.

They assume the forms should be capable of being filled out by any lay person. This is hogwash. The forms are a mess.

There is another reason, however, why family law lends itself to limited legal services. By definition, when a client limits legal services, he takes greater responsibility for the strategy and conduct of the legal proceeding. What legal relationship is more personal than one involving your family? As the consumer movement hits the legal world, it is not surprising that the first area where people demand greater control and autonomy involves intimate decisions concerning their marriages and their children.

Add to this mix the fact that the courts and legislatures have failed miserably to address the needs of families in the late 20TH century, and a perfect vacuum has been created for innovation in legal services. No, I don't mean that legislatures are evil; they have just lost focus on the main problem. Most legislators are not lawyers and the ones who are rarely have experience in family law. They tend to respond to whatever special interest group is hot this year. Each time legislatures meet and try to address the latest problem by adding another rule, family law procedures are rendered ever more cumbersome. This makes it harder and harder to obtain a simple uncontested divorce at a reasonable cost. The lawyers who want to provide low cost legal services (and there are many who do) cannot because the legislature insists that they jump through all sorts of unnecessary hoops and fill out stupid and time consuming forms. They are forced to charge for all of this because, of course, the staff who do the paperwork have to be paid, and we have a vicious circle.

At the same time, family law judges are being asked to handle a volume of cases that would be considered ludicrous in any other area of the law. Every year, thousands, literally tens of thousands of cases are pushed through the family courts of this country in which someone's entire estate, support rights, sometimes even custody are decided in the equivalent of about 20 minutes to an hour of court time. Of course it is absurd; it is also true. And don't look for hundreds of new courts to be funded by the tax-payers in order to pick up the slack, either. In most areas, we can't even get school bonds passed as more and more Americans determine they are over-taxed to pay for the government they already have. This means that we can't expect the courts to become substantially more responsive in the short term.

Instead, people are being forced to find new ways to resolve their family problems with minimal involvement by courts and attorneys.

Who's Right is it to Decide How Much Your Lawyer Has to Do?

This was *your* marriage and it is your divorce. They are your kids, your house and your pots and pans. I should note here that I am using the plural "you." Each of you comes with a spouse, who has exactly the same rights and vested interests. If you choose to exercise those rights, congratulations. But don't forget that you are still only one of two parties to a proceeding, not supreme dictator. Presumably, your goal in limiting legal services is that you want your divorce to be less litigious, not more so. However, take a good look in the mirror. If the real reason you want to represent yourself with a coach in the background is so you can continue to direct your families' lives and can't bear giving up control, you are doomed to disappointment.

Whose Responsibility is it?

As more and more family law litigants seek to limit legal services, they are forced to wrestle with this question. In the "old" days, you hired a lawyer who would set the strategy and tell you when to be at court, what to say, what to do and, at the end would hand you your divorce papers. The client's role was essentially passive: to provide the attorney with information as requested. The judge decided who got what, where the kids lived and how much support was paid.

If you want to reassert your right to participate in those decisions, you simply must be willing to accept responsibility for the consequences. In some ways, it is very easy to let the judge decide: you don't have to take responsibility for making a bad decision, and if you are unhappy with the result, you have someone else to blame.

This really has been the way of the American legal system. We give power over our lives to strangers, then complain that they did not use it properly. If you want to assume the responsibility, then do so, but be clean about it.

Why is it Important?

If we want the courts to meet our needs as citizens, we must demand it of them. That includes providing them with the resources required to meet those demands. A case in point is court funding. The courts are lamenting that their budgets are being squeezed ever tighter, and I know this to be true. At the same time, taxpayers are refusing to vote additional taxes to build more courts. While this hurts in the short term, I believe it is a good thing in the long run. What the taxpayers are saying is that they are not willing to make the financial commitment necessary to build the courtrooms which would be required if everyone who wanted a divorce (or had any other legal problem, for that matter) surrendered their power to the courts. They may not understand it in this way, but the choice to limit court funding is forcing us to look at new and constructive ways to handle family problems outside the traditional court system.

If you want to minimize the power that the judge and attorneys have over your life, then you should consider being on the cutting edge yourself and entering into an agreement for limited legal services. However, before you can make such a decision, you must have thought it through yourself. You must educate yourself about what will need to be done in your case and the technical (and frankly emotional) difficulty of taking on some or most of it yourself. You must clearly understand the risks and benefits of the course you are adopting. You will not be able to give clear instructions to your attorney or properly evaluate the tasks to be delegated unless you have done the analysis which follows. Therefore, it is critical that you read through the guidelines and make sure that you understand the risks and benefits of each of the available options so that your decisions are informed ones. Read the text, then work through the appendices, referring back to the text as necessary to fully answer the questions.

Get Informed

An essential element is the initial evaluation of the legal issues presented by the case. This must be done by competent legal counsel. It stands to reason: how can you know what to delegate and what to do yourself if you don't know the legal consequences of each? Therefore, spend the money on a consultation with a qualified attorney, and don't get cheap about it. This isn't the time to insist only on meeting with an attorney who offers "free initial consultation." After all, in most cases the reason the initial conference is free is because the attorney hopes to sign you up for later services. If you truly want and intend to unbundle, make sure there are no hidden agendas working. Otherwise you may find yourself distrusting the advice you receive. Pay for the conference and be up front about the fact that you are considering limited legal services. Then, if you are told your case has to be litigated, you will be more comfortable that the opinion is based on the facts and law of your case, rather than because the attorney needs to recoup the cost of the consultation. I'm not saying that all attorneys who advertise free initial consultations will lead you down the primrose path; quite the contrary. On the other hand, be realistic about it. You are better off telling the attorney at the outset that you intend to pay for his time, are seriously considering limited legal services, and want the advice to include the consequences of doing so.[2]

Definitions

There are a number of terms which will need to be defined for purposes of the following discussion.

We start with the premise of the "traditional" approach to family law, sometimes called "full service." This was drilled into lawyers in law school, tattooed into their hides by malpractice insurance carriers, and the Big Brother of the State Bar Association. It says that when a client retains an attorney, the attorney is responsible for every facet of the case. In family law, that means identifying and dividing the property, litigating custody and visitation disputes, identifying income and obtaining appropriate support awards, both child support and alimony, and using reasonable diligence to locate concealed or missing assets. They are told that it is a breach of ethics for them to do any less than all of it, *even if the client instructs them otherwise.* Presumably this is based on the paternalistic theory that litigants are too stupid to make their own decisions or know when legal protections can be safely waived.

So, what happens when you consult an attorney on a case in which the estate is modest, but there is real concern about custody? Suppose there is little property and the support issues are minimal, but your spouse is a substance abuser and you are worried about the kids. The estate clearly doesn't warrant the full service approach, and you don't want the attorney to address anything but custody. Under the traditional system, the attorney may agree with your assessment of the case. Nevertheless, he takes the risk that the State Bar will discipline him or the malpractice insurance carrier will deny coverage if he does not insist on doing the pots and pans as well (and, of course, billing for the time).

---

[2]Check out Appendix 4 on questions to ask your attorney and Appendix 1 on the issues presented by your case.

Many attorneys agree that this is nuts. They don't feel good about performing unnecessary services, and hate the poor client relations which inevitably result. Some of them respond by actively offering and promoting limited legal services. Different terms are used, however, and if you are going to communicate clearly, you must understand them.

Unbundling[3]

This is my favorite term for limiting legal services because it is so descriptive. The concept is that the traditional approach requires attorneys to offer a bundle of services, consisting of all aspects of the case. Unbundling means that the attorney and the client can agree that the attorney will provide some, but not all, of the services contained in a classic family law case. After discussing the issues presented by your case and the options available with an attorney, you instruct her on which specific tasks she is to perform, and take the responsibility for others. Lines of demarcation are drawn and the attorney assumes responsibility (and liability) only for those areas which you and she agree on. If you instruct her not to get involved in property, she will not do so. It is then your responsibility if you do not like the property division which results.

I'll spend a great deal more time discussing unbundling and some of the countless ways in which it can be structured in later chapters and the appendices. There are infinite variations which a thoughtful and creative attorney and client can use to define their relationship if they so choose. What is important here is to know that the concept is fluid and not only can, but *must* be tailored to the needs of an individual case and litigant.

Limited Legal Services

Although more of a mouthful, this is basically the same as unbundling. It means that the client and attorney contract with

---

[3]This term was coined by Forrest S. Mosten, one of the national leaders in increasing the accessibility of legal services. He's got his own book coming out soon. Watch for it.

each other for the attorney to provide some, but not all, of the traditional legal services. The client instructs the attorney not to perform certain services and releases him from liability for those which the client wants to handle himself. As with unbundling, the issues in the case must be clearly defined, the client must be advised of consequences of assuming responsibility for certain areas, and both sides need to be absolutely clear on the parameters of their respective responsibility and authority. Other terms which mean the same thing are limited scope representation and discrete services representation.

Consulting Attorneys

Consulting attorneys may never be retained at all. This simply means that you periodically check in with the attorney to make sure you understand your legal rights or the court procedures, but you are basically on your own. This arrangement is frequently associated with a mediated divorce, from which the practice grew. In recent years, the number of couples electing to mediate their divorces rather than opt for the traditional approach has grown exponentially. They see this as preferable to litigation as a solution to their divorce problems.

Most mediators refuse to give legal advice to either party and insist that each has his or her own consulting attorney. In this way, each party is apprised of the legal consequences of proposed agreements at every stage of the mediation. Both parties are on equal footing in the negotiations by being assured of the same access to financial and other data, as well as knowledge of the legal consequences of the various options available to them. It also insures that each party to the mediation knows what he or she is bargaining for before signing on the dotted line.

A consulting attorney may or may not prepare paperwork to be filed by the court. She will advise the client on the legal issues presented by the specific case, and perhaps suggest alternative approaches to resolution. She is responsible for the quality of the advice she gives on specific topics, but not for handling all aspects of the case.

The same approach can be used outside the mediation model. You may choose to represent yourself in all phases of the litigation, and simply want to consult from time to time so you will be aware of legal or procedural pitfalls. You pay for the time you are with the attorney, and go away.

Coaching

More and more litigants are looking for an attorney to coach them. You may want to represent yourself, but obviously need to know the law and procedures. However, if you are doing it all yourself rather than relying on a mediator, you may want more than just a simple narrative lesson on the law from your attorney. Instead, you may ask to be instructed in technique, strategy, and all the options available to you. You also need to know about the applicable court procedures. *Pro se* litigants are bound by the same rules as lawyers. Your papers must be filed in the same manner and in the same form, the same time deadlines apply and most judges do not significantly relax the rules. Therefore, as a *pro se* litigant you will want to have a resource to whom you can turn to learn the court procedures and deadlines; otherwise, you may be deprived of substantive rights for failure to comply with a technical rule.

A coach is likely to give specific pointers on procedures, negotiation techniques, what to expect from a particular judge, how to get the case on calendar, how to present evidence, how to draft declarations and the like. This is very much a "how to do it yourself" relationship rather than a sharing of responsibility. The coach is teaching you how to deal with specific issues which you have identified; he is not stepping in and doing it for you.

What About Paralegal Services?

Some of you will decide to use a paralegal service to prepare your divorce paperwork. There are times when this is a good choice, but beware of the pitfalls. Most paralegal services simply help you fill out forms. This may be all you need if you *already know* all the legal issues presented by your case because you have consulted with a lawyer. However, paralegals are not qualified to give legal advice because they aren't trained to do so. Most will respect the line between assisting with paperwork and giving legal advice, but some will not. I have seen too many people overlook serious issues because they relied on a paralegal to tell them their rights and remedies. This is always a mistake. In some states, it is even a crime to practice law without a license. The risk to you as the client is that you will miss an important issue because it *seems* simple to you. It is money well spent to consult with an experienced attorney about your rights before assuming it is safe to depend on a paralegal service.

Before deciding to use a paralegal service, find out the qualifications of the paralegal you are considering. Appendix 5 at page 69 contains a list of suggested questions.

There are generally two ways in which a paralegal is trained. One is to complete a formal training program and obtain a certificate. This may include specialized training in family law procedures and internships where they work in an office and learn the ropes. In other cases, it consists of nothing more than an overview of lots of areas of law, with little or no emphasis on family law. If the latter, they may have little practical experience in what you want them to do.

The other training ground is in a traditional law firm. Many paralegals have developed expertise in complex family law discovery and tracing, or in dealing with complicated pension issues. Then, after getting sick and tired of the rigidity and rigmarole which pervades many law firms, they strike out on their own, taking their expertise with them. Find out which category your prospective paralegal falls into before entrusting your estate to him.

Don't forget, also, that paralegals do not carry malpractice insurance. Therefore, if they give you bad advice and you rely on it to your detriment, you probably have no recourse.

How Do You Decide?

As a litigant you will have to understand and analyze the issues presented by your case before you can evaluate which, if any, of these approaches would be most appropriate for you. The discussion which follows will outline a process whereby you can determine whether your situation is amenable to some form of unbundling and, if so, what form that should take.

2

Are You a Good Candidate for Limited Legal Services?

How can you tell?

I will later discuss in detail the myriad ways in which legal services can be limited, either by the specific task to be performed or the subject matter area. However, before you can get to the question of which unbundling structure will work best for you, you need to address a much more important threshold question: Are *you* a good candidate for limited legal services?

Emotional Overload

Are you able to detach yourself enough from the obvious emotional content of your divorce in order to make clear decisions about your property, support or children? This is the first threshold issue, and Appendix 7 starting at page 75 contains a detailed self test questionnaire to help you analyze it.

One of the most important functions of lawyers or mediators in divorce is to superimpose an independent, objective and emotionally uninvolved view of the case. Now, let's not kid ourselves: *of course* you can't be totally uninvolved. It's your divorce, for crying out loud. But if you can't at least see that and attempt to separate a logical or financial decision from its emotional content, you simply will not be a good candidate for limited legal representation. You will be unable to see when it is preferable to concede an issue you can't win and concentrate on one you can. You may go to war and draw a line in the sand over a matter of little overall importance. If you or your spouse has defined a minor issue as the benchmark of the cosmic win/lose dynamic, investing it with lots of emotional baggage, someone has to be around to point that out to you. Otherwise, you'll just make a fool of yourself and lose credibility with the judge. You must have someone whom you trust, who is knowledgeable about your case, and who can provide an independent perspective for you.[1]

The reality is that if it makes you nuts to have to deal with your spouse over what time the kids are due back from soccer practice, you may not be emotionally equipped to negotiate the bigger issues with him. You aren't ahead if the money you would have spent on legal fees is paid to your therapist instead.

Ideally, you and your spouse both agree that it is in the best interests of all concerned, including the kids, to detach from the emotional content as much as possible. You may not always succeed, but it makes both of you better candidates for unbundling.

Can You Handle the Paperwork?

Let's face it: Legal paperwork is technical and confusing. Even lawyers and paralegals sometimes struggle with it. If you really cannot do it (and we are not all Rhodes scholars) be honest and acknowledge it. You may be able to find a paralegal to draft it for you or you may prefer to leave this on the list of your attorney's responsibilities. Representing yourself involves not only court forms, complex financial disclosures and expense statements, but business letters, subpoenas and court orders. In addition, you may have to prepare written court exhibits to prove your side of the case. You won't win at trial if your "evidence" is a shopping bag full of papers which you rifle through between

---

[1]And *don't* assume your best friend or a family member can do this for you. First, it isn't a fair burden to impose on a personal relationship. Second, your friend probably has her own agenda and attitudes about divorce which may not be the same as yours.

questions. If your case involves documentary evidence and you are not good at organizing it in an orderly fashion, find someone to do this for you.

Be realistic: If you are freaked out by a legal form or agonize for days about writing a simple letter, you are probably not a good candidate to fill out the disclosures.

Is There History of Verbal or Physical Abuse in Your Family?

Is your mate used to being in control and having all edicts automatically obeyed?

If so, this is not for you. These patterns do not go away just because you are divorcing, and you are likely to be taken advantage of again without a strong advocate in your corner. Think about it: Can you effectively stand up for your rights in a settlement meeting when you are scared to death your mate will ram your car as you pull out of the parking lot (or worse)? If your spouse has been telling you for the last 20 years that you are stupid, incompetent, and have not had a sensible idea since birth, and you've started to believe him, are you really going to effectively counter his arguments with reasoned defenses of your own? The answer may be yes, but don't be surprised if, despite the best will (and coaching) in the world, the old patterns reassert themselves. If this is the case, you are better off leaving the negotiation and court appearances to someone else.

Is Your Spouse a Crook?

Now, some of you may say yes, because he looked elsewhere for love, thereby violating the marriage vows, but that's not what I'm talking about. That may have nothing whatsoever to do with your ability to represent yourself. If you are just jealous, it is probably irrelevant to the question of whether you need a full service divorce or can handle part of it yourself. (Although it is highly relevant to whether you can emotionally detach enough to make good decisions about your case.)[2]

On the other hand, if the reason you answered yes is because he took great pleasure in hiding income from the IRS for 25 years and was infinitely creative in his attempts, you probably will need to take advantage of all of the protections the law affords. After all, that's what they are there for. You certainly should not take his word for where the money is, or rely on your best guess to turn up the missing assets. This also isn't the best time to try to learn how to draft a technical subpoena to be sure you get the right information. Get help.

Are You Comfortable Handling Financial Issues or Going Through Stacks of Bank Records?

Many people aren't, and will probably need assistance if they are going to be successful in these areas. In divorce, some of the greatest pitfalls are financial. If you have never handled the money in your family, have no knowledge of investments and are intimidated by financial records, it is going to be difficult for you to find the missing assets, trace the separate contribution to the joint property, or to assess (or make) a settlement offer, because you just won't have the skills. This is not a criticism, because many very intelligent people have routinely relied on others to do these things. The point is, however, that if you have relied on someone else (especially your spouse) to do this for you, don't expect to become a financial planning wizard overnight. Look at it this way: You can learn, but do you really want to practice on your own divorce and risk your financial future? Remember, divorce is at best a period of considerable emotional distress, and it may not be the ideal time for you to acquire advanced training in finance and negotiation.

---

[2]Check out the self test in Appendix 7 and the goals questionnaire in Appendix 8 and answer both of them honestly and completely in writing.

If this describes you, have someone assist you in evaluating your financial estate, support rights and settlement offers, as well as analyzing the documents. This may be a consulting attorney, maybe an unbundled attorney or someone doing a full service divorce. However, it is essential that you clearly and dispassionately evaluate yourself and your own abilities before assuming that you are equipped to do the financial analysis without professional assistance.

Are You Decisive?

Many of the decisions you will be called upon to make during your divorce are irrevocable. You can't just try on a property settlement for size to see how you like it. The decisions you will be forced to make have consequences which are not easily undone, if at all. How frightening is this to you?

Many people have no difficulty making the routine decisions of life, but are utterly paralyzed when required to make an irrevocable decision, or simply commit to a financial course of action. Incidentally, this has nothing to do with intelligence or lack thereof; it is a function of personality type. If you are terrified you might make the wrong decision, and always suspect that the other side must know something that you don't, you'll probably make no decision at all. That is almost invariably disastrous.

Let me illustrate a common pattern: only rarely do decisions all arise at the same time in a divorce. Typically, you will have to make decisions on an ongoing basis as the case proceeds. You can't always wait to see the "big picture" with all pieces neatly in place before having to commit to something irrevocable. Perhaps the issue is whether to sell the house. If you can't decide whether to sell the house before you know what the support order will be, but can't set the support before you know how much money comes out of the house, you've got a chicken and egg problem. *Nothing* at all is resolved because you can't know all the possible consequences. As a result, you might lose the opportunity to craft a good solution.

The point is that if you are so afraid of making a wrong decision that you make none at all, you will undercut your own position at every turn. If you find making decisions distressing, or tend to constantly second guess yourself thereafter, think twice about trying to go it alone.

Are You Good With Details and Follow Through ?

Again, many people are not. They may be great at evaluating the "big picture," but deadlines and details somehow slip through the cracks. This can be devastating when missing the deadline means you have lost the opportunity to present your side of the case to the judge. At trial, you will be a sitting duck for a well organized opponent.

As with so much else in life, the rule here is *know thyself*, and if these are not among your aptitudes, find someone else whose strengths compensate for your weaknesses.

Do You Think of Yourself as a Victim?

If so, don't even try to represent yourself. I don't mean to sound insensitive, but those patterns don't go away overnight. If you answered yes, you will just be setting yourself up to be a victim all over again, and in spades. Instead, work on the victim thing in counseling. If you get to the point where you feel in charge and want to take responsibility (including responsibility for the consequences if they don't go your way) then maybe you can take on more of the case yourself later.

Similarly, if you look to the litigation process as an opportunity to "get even" for past wrongs, you will not be effective. You will lack the necessary emotional detachment, and your private agenda will bleed through into every aspect of the proceeding.

Get Real About the Time Commitment

Most people don't have a clue how much time it takes to effectively prepare and present a divorce case. They get the attorney's bill and can't *believe* that it took that much time to prepare the motion. Trust me: It will take the unrepresented party ten times as long if not more, at least if you are going to do it well.

If you have primary responsibility for the children, getting your life in order, coping with the emotional consequences of divorce, possibly retraining or starting a new job *and* learning the law and procedures, doing the paperwork and preparing your case for trial, guess what it is likely to get short shrift? There are simply not enough hours in the day to do it properly under those circumstances.

Suppose you are the CEO of a major corporation. You are probably very comfortable making important business decisions, analyzing financial situations quickly and accurately, and taking full responsibility for the consequences. But do you really have the time to do it properly in your divorce? If your work is going to suffer radically, you had better have help. It is cheap at the price if it keeps you from running your business into the ground because your mind and attention are elsewhere.

Even if you have a very simple case, it may be that you are just not equipped either emotionally, intellectually or due to the stress of the divorce or the time commitment to undertake even part of your own representation. If so, try to make the best decision that you can about hiring a lawyer and make sure you don't run up unnecessary costs and fees.[3]

If, on the other hand, you have clearly assessed your strengths and weaknesses, including your ability to take responsibility for the consequences of your own decisions, read on. We will now begin to explore the different ways in which legal services can be limited and how you can find just the right person to compensate for your weaknesses while taking full advantage of your strengths.

---

[3]A good resource is my earlier book, *How to Avoid the Divorce From Hell (and dance together at your daughter's wedding)*, which provides a basic education on what the courts can and cannot do for you, and how to make the best of the system.

3

Where To Start Limiting Representation

What Kind of Case Do You Have?

Before we start talking about delegation of duties between you and your legal representative, you need to understand precisely what work your case requires to be adequately prepared and presented. It stands to reason: How can you start apportioning tasks effectively if you do not know what they are?

The first thing to do is determine which issues are going to be important in your case. Before answering the checklist in Appendix 1 starting on page 55, consider the following:

Support

What is the source of the money available for support? It makes a huge difference if it is fixed W-2 income which varies little from month to month or a family-run business where the income fluctuates widely. If the pay stubs provide a fairly good picture of the actual income in the family, very little investigation is going to be required. On the other hand, if there is a business where personal expenses are routinely paid through a business account or credit card, significantly more leg work is necessary.

Are there support guidelines in your state? If so, are they done by computer? In this case, you are almost certain to require some knowledgeable person to run the computer programs for you. This entails much more than being able to turn on the computer and having a passing familiarity with the software. As with any other computer process, garbage in equals garbage out. If you don't know how the tax assumptions work, you can't input the correct figures. In that case, you will not get a representative support number, no matter how many times you run the program.

Is marital standard of living important in your case or in your state? If so, this may be one of the things you need help in developing. Evidence of marital standard of living is notoriously difficult to gather, quantify and present effectively to the court.

House

The relative difficulty of the house issue is rarely a function just of value. An expensive house can be a minor and very simple issue if it is being sold and the proceeds divided equally. On the other hand, an inexpensive house may present serious complications if one party is asking for an unequal share or there are serious tax issues. What if one or the other of you put family money into it or there is a huge capital gain problem? What if some of the down payment came from your mate's parents and they want it back? You may need help on this one.

Pensions

If you have always worked with the same company and are near retirement, this may be a no-brainer. However, what if there is a carry over from prior employer? Stock options? A 401(k) or company savings plan? Early retirement incentives? Not so simple. You may require an actuary to help evaluate pensions and will almost certainly need to consult with an attorney to alert you to the legal issues lurking in that deceptively simple employee benefit statement you get every year from the retirement plan.

If you need a Qualified Domestic Relations Order to protect your interest in the pension, you will almost certainly need help with it. Ask your attorney about this.

Quicksand Issues

These are the things that look simple on the surface. However, in the infinite wisdom of our legal system, we have added layers and layers of complexity. I could not begin to detail them all, and there is amazing diversity from state to state.

For example, in some states, the date of separation is infinitely important, and the result can make a huge difference in the size of the marital estate. This can be one of the trickiest issues around, and don't assume that it is the day that someone moves in to separate bedrooms (or sometimes even to a separate house!) There are many factors to be evaluated and lots of potential traps.

In some states, fault is still an issue and definitions of the conduct which constitute fault change with the phases of the moon. Again, what seems like fault to *you* doesn't necessarily meet the legal standard. It is essential that you consult with an attorney (and tell her *everything* just to ensure that there aren't any of these nasty issues lurking out there) before you decide to dispense with her assistance.

Custody

Here is the biggie. Almost no one has sufficient detachment to effectively represent himself in a custody dispute. Sorry, but that's the way it is. And frankly, would you really *want* to be able to emotionally detach from it anyway? Of course not; they're your kids. If custody is going to be fully litigated in your case, make sure that you have an independent custody expert with whom you are, at the very least, consulting and preferably one who presents the evidence in court. This is not one I would take chances with.

The bottom line is that it is almost impossible to represent yourself effectively in your own custody case. Even the best custody lawyer in the state will do a lousy job in his own case because he is emotionally involved. I've seen it happen.

The Consequences of Being "Of Record"

Each of the preceding discussions assumes that you and your attorney will divide responsibility for the case on an issue by issue basis. This works best if there is one area of overriding importance and the other areas are relatively minor. It doesn't work if several issues are to be fully litigated.

When a case is litigated, the court will want to know who is "of record." That means that someone (usually the attorney) is designated to be the one to receive official notices from the court and opposing party, and to appear and present your case at settlement conferences and hearings. Few, if any, courts will allow two people to be "of record" at the same time. I have never seen a judge who will allow an attorney to present part of a trial and the client to present another part. That's just the way it is. If you have to present and litigate several issues, there may be no choice but for you to be "of record" of all of them, even if you are being coached behind the scenes.

Unbundling Horizontally[4]

The prior discussion assumes that you can divide responsibility for your case on an issue by issue basis. Suppose the case does not break down by subject matter, custody versus support, property and pension. Suppose instead that it lends itself to assigning some of the tasks to the lawyer and keeping some for yourself. This means that one of you would do all of the discovery, for example, whether it applied to property, support, or custody.

---

[4]Those of you with training in early American history will instantly think of a quaint colonial courting custom. No, that is not what we're talking about here.

Someone else would be responsible for all of the negotiations or the court appearances, regardless of the issue at stake.

Some of the ways to break down the case horizontally are as follows:

Discovery

Essentially, this is nothing more than fact gathering. It can be informal, highly technical or anything in between. How it develops in your case will impact whether or not you need the assistance of an attorney or paralegal to pursue discovery.

Informal discovery is just that: You and your spouse share the information available to each of you so that you can make informed decisions. If there is a high level of trust, this may be all you need and you can proceed to the next step.

If there isn't, however, you may need to do formal discovery. This can run the gamut from sending subpoenas to taking depositions. I will be honest with you. It is tough for a non-lawyer to take a really good deposition, even with excellent coaching. This is just one of those skills which take lawyers years to develop. On the other hand, if all you really need are the records, under some circumstances that may be done as easily by a paralegal as an attorney.[5] Most good attorneys have paralegals who do a great deal of the nuts and bolts discovery. The reason is obvious: Discovery is tedious and time consuming, except in the simplest of cases. It would be prohibitively expensive if the attorney did it all, and in many cases would be a waste of his time and training. With proper direction a good paralegal (who has *extensive family law discovery experience*[6]) may do just as well.

If you decide that you need help with discovery, should it be an attorney or a paralegal? The answer depends on how complex the issues are. If you are tracing stock options or some other asset

---

[5]See Appendices 4 and 5 about questions to ask lawyers and paralegals.

[6]See more about this in the section of Chapter 2 on paralegal services.

which is highly technical, I would want an attorney involved, and a very good one. Frankly, a lot of family lawyers don't know jack about stock options. If you are tracing joint and separate funds which have been commingled over the years, you may be able to use a forensic accountant or even a highly experienced family law paralegal. For years I had a paralegal who was a whiz at tracing and discovery, but many are not. Ask about their experience. A paralegal degree does not necessarily mean that she has experience in the issues you need help with, and not all accountants are specialists in divorce accounting and tracing. Both are extremely technical fields.

Whatever your decision about who should take the laboring oar for discovery, remember that you are still the best source for information. You will know things about the family finances that your attorney or paralegal could not possibly know. Therefore, even if you don't send out the subpoenas, you *must* go through the records yourself. There will be names or other information which will trigger a lead in you that would be meaningless to anyone else.

Negotiation

Any divorce is going to require at least an attempt at negotiation. By definition, only a lunatic would prefer going to trial to settling out of court, and even if your mate is a nut, you will want to at least attempt a negotiated settlement. After all, the whole purpose of this exercise is to minimize the time, expense and angst necessary to get the piece of paper that says you are divorced.

The truth is that most people are not skilled negotiators. In fact, many attorneys are not either, but that is a different subject and don't get me started. Even good negotiators are lousy when negotiating their own case, for the obvious reason of personal involvement. There is a huge difference between negotiating a widget contract with ABC corporation, and negotiating a divorce settlement with someone you slept with for years. Not only is the emotional content different; so are the rules. I once represented one of the most savvy and successful business negotiators in the country. He kept trying to run the negotiations like he did his last international contract. It didn't work. Fortunately, he realized it in time. After seriously misreading the negotiations for a while, he was smart enough to recognize that the tactics which were so successful for him in business negotiations were totally ineffective with his extremely angry ex-wife. He turned the negotiations over to me and we settled the case. I am sure I couldn't have negotiated some of the high powered international contracts he has. On the other hand, divorce negotiation is my forte and I am not emotionally invested in the result.

If you decide you want an attorney to negotiate for you, you have to spend some time (and money) educating her on every facet of the case that you've handled yourself. Obviously, you don't want her to go to the bargaining table with only some of the cards while your opponent is holding a full hand. In negotiations, you never know when some minor nugget of information is just the leverage you need to get the concession you want. It is well worth the price. The last thing you want is to hire someone to negotiate for you, but get cheap about educating her on your side of the case. That just guarantees that you will lose, not because of lack of negotiating skill, but lack of vital information.

Court Appearances

If you feel comfortable doing your own investigation and fact gathering, but throw up at the thought of standing up in front of a crowded courtroom (and no, they are *not* private), you may want to hire an attorney solely to appear in court for you. After a while, if you find yourself returning to court repeatedly, you might become confident enough to do it on your own. However, I doubt that someone who is so terrified that their voice can barely be heard is going to be an effective advocate for any legal position, however meritorious it may be.

Drafting

Ask any lawyer: Drafting can be tricky. This includes legal briefs and affidavits. The good news is that drafting is one of the easiest legal services to unbundle.[7]

Drafting may be important even if you don't have any issues complicated enough to require detailed legal briefs. For example, you will probably have to file declarations or affidavits at some point in your case. Most non-lawyers don't have a clue how to prepare them. They fill them with hearsay and personal attacks on the character of their mate, all of which is emotionally gratifying but legally irrelevant. Since you are asking the court to rule in your favor, the last thing you want is for your valid arguments to be lost in a sea of venom about what a rat your spouse is. The likely result of that kind of affidavit is that the judge is going to blow it off. Therefore, one of the best uses of your attorney's time may be to draft the affidavit or to review the one you have written and edit out the extraneous material.

One of the best uses of limited legal services is the drafting of orders. The wording of orders must be extremely precise. Perhaps you can do this yourself and only need the attorney to look it over. However, you may want to have the attorney prepare the order, even if you represented yourself at the hearing.

An order is going to be the most important piece of paper in any legal proceeding. Not only does it memorialize for all time what the judge said everybody had to do, but it will periodically need to be enforced or perhaps modified in the future. It is highly likely that the judge who will be called upon to interpret, enforce or modify the order is not the one who granted it. Even if it is, she's probably heard hundreds if not thousands of cases in between and will be unlikely to remember precisely what she meant if the order is unclear. Worse, a perceived ambiguity is likely to be resolved in favor of the one trying to weasel out of the

---

[7]Check out the discussion of ghostwriting and scripting in Chapter 4.

order. Therefore, if there is the slightest uncertainty about what was meant, you may find that the order you thought you had goes up in smoke. Any attorney who has tried to enforce an ambiguous or badly drafted order will have useful suggestions on how to tighten up the language and plug loopholes. That may make all the difference in whether or not you actually receive the relief you thought you won. It doesn't take long for an attorney to review an order which you have drafted and it can save you thousands of dollars in later enforcement proceedings.

Legal Research

This one is obvious. Lawyers spend years learning to do legal research and writing, and you probably won't have time to learn it as you go through your divorce. He can save you a huge amount of time by directing you to the best sources for your kind of case, or researching and writing the briefs for you.

A few lawyers have client libraries where you can do your own research, including computerized support guidelines, case books and other legal resources. Some charge an hourly rate for the use of their library, while others do not. They generally will not let you check books out because they need them for the next client. However, if your attorney does have a client library, he may direct you to the most useful sources and you may be able to do some of the research yourself. Be prepared, however, to spend at least five times as long as the attorney would to find the same information, simply because he is familiar with it and you are not.

How you ultimately decide to break down the legal services is up to you and your attorney, dictated by the comfort level of each of you and the specific issues and difficulties presented by your case. Custody may not be a problem at all and you may be very comfortable doing your own investigation and legwork. However, you may want an attorney to actually appear at the settlement conferences and court appearances with you. On the other hand, the pension may be the most important component of your estate, and you may want an attorney to do all of the investigation, discovery, drafting and research on that issue, while you take care of everything else yourself.

The permutations are endless and limited only by your creativity and willingness and that of your attorney.

4

How To Find an Attorney Who Will Work With You

Most of you will not be surprised to hear that many attorneys are reluctant to offer unbundled legal services. However, you *will* be surprised at the reasons.

State Bar Pressure

In some states, the State Bar Association (which can be a bureaucracy not unlike the federal government) is going through a period of split personality. On the one hand, they admonish attorneys that it is our ethical duty to expand the availability of legal services. From the other side of their mouths, the enforcement arm is simultaneously traveling up and down the state telling family lawyers that unbundling is a no-no, and if they do it, they are jeopardizing their professional licenses. The irony (not to mention utter absurdity) of this position is lost on all but a few.

Why are they being so myopic? Well, for starters, most of the lawyers who work for the state bar *have never practiced law!* That's right, folks. They are administrators and bureaucrats who have never been in the trenches. They have never had to explain to a client why they are required to perform and charge him for legal services which both of them agree are unnecessary, just because the rules say so. They never had to explain to a client why, as a result of the hundreds of cases and the phony baloney rules which are being applied to each, it will take months to get into court to obtain a support or custody order. Or why it is necessary to jump through hoops which are obviously irrelevant to the facts of your case, just because the legislature made a rule to correct a problem in another kind of case.

Why does this happen? Well, the long answer would take a book of its own.[1] Disclosure statutes are a case in point. Some people conceal assets and defraud their spouse by not disclosing all possible assets or business opportunities. As a result, the legislature has decreed that before a divorce can be granted in California, very complicated, time consuming and expensive forms must be prepared and exchanged in order to protect litigants from possible fraud. But what if you know there has been full disclosure, and don't want to go to the trouble or spend the money? This is a perfect example of what is wrong with the legislative mentality: because *some* low life will defraud his spouse and conceal assets, we have invented a rule which will require *everyone* to fill out an expensive set of forms, even if they *know* there is nothing hidden. The court can't grant a divorce without it, and up goes the ante again. And no, this is not the Family Lawyer's Financial Relief Act. Most of them hate it. They went nuts because the earliest form of the rule wasn't even waivable. This meant that even if you and your spouse agreed that the disclosure forms were irrelevant and a waste of time and money, you couldn't opt out of the requirement. *Say what? The legislature thinks we are so incapable of protecting ourselves from each other that it takes from us even the power to waive protections that don't apply to us.* As a result, a rule which is designed to prevent a limited number of fraudulent bad guys from taking advantage of credulous spouses adds hundreds, maybe thousands of dollars to the minimum cost of a divorce in the state of California. And why are we surprised that people don't want to pay for it and prefer to limit their cost by limiting the lawyer's involvement?

---

[1] Its in process. The working title is *Broken Justice: the Failure of Family Law.* Watch for it.

This is where many state bar associations jump in and decree that lawyers are ethically required to handle all aspects of every case which they accept. Now, it is clear that this rule might make sense in some cases. In a criminal case, it is inconceivable that the defense attorney would be retained to handle the investigation but not the trial, or the burglary counts but not the charge for possession of stolen property. Likewise, in an automobile accident, it would be ludicrous for the plaintiff's attorney to represent the plaintiff's interest against driver of the car but not the owner.

Another case in point is ghostwriting or scripting. Many clients who want to represent themselves will consult with an attorney to script their testimony questions or ghostwrite letters and pleadings. This is fine in some states. However, the California State Bar has issued an ethics opinion saying it is a breach of ethics for an attorney to script questions or ghostwrite pleadings. Many judges across the country take the position that an attorney who ghostwrites documents is perpetrating "a fraud on the court" which could result in sanctions. While this sorry state is not the case in all courts, it is still a prevalent judicial mindset. As a result, attorneys who sincerely want to help by scripting questions for testimony or drafting pleadings under the client's name may be jeopardizing their professional licenses in some states.

These rules simply don't graft comfortably onto a family law system. Nevertheless, the State Bar has its paradigm (read: tunnel vision) and does not seem to understand that different kinds of cases require different approaches. A few enlightened souls appreciate the need for change, but reform moveth slowly. In the meantime, many family lawyers who very much want to offer limited legal services to their clients are scared to death that they will jeopardize their professional license and livelihood thereby, not to mention their kid's orthodontia.

However, the State Bar is not the only culprit.

Malpractice Insurance Carriers

This is good one. If it weren't so real and so harmful, I would laugh.

Most lawyers carry malpractice insurance to protect themselves against the inevitable "oops!". Remember, none of us is perfect. However, when something slips through the cracks, someone is going to get sued. That's fine. That's what the coverage is there for. The problem arises when the insurance carrier says "no coverage if you unbundle."

You would think they would have learned from the mediation experience. Years ago, when mediation was new and untried, some carriers denied coverage, or even raised rates, because they thought liability would increase. The reverse happened. People were so happy with the results they obtained themselves with the assistance of their mediator that claims *decreased*. What a surprise. People are happier when they are treated like grownups and given the tools to craft their own solutions. Now, most malpractice insurance rates for mediators are lower than for traditional family law attorneys.

Do you think our friendly local malpractice insurance carriers learned from the experience? Guess again. This means that even if the lawyer agrees that the case does not justify his involvement in all issues, he may be reluctant to limit his services for fear that the insurance carrier will deny coverage. The upshot is that the insurance carriers set the "standard of care," in effect legislating what an attorney can or cannot do for you, even if you both agree that it is nuts.

Remember too, that the lawyer has bills to pay and college expenses to fund. Many of them are just not comfortable with unbundling legal services and risking their insurance coverage. The good news is that a growing number are not only willing to do it, but pledging themselves to actively promote limited services. You may have to shop around to find one, however.

The irony of all of this is that experience has demonstrated that as with mediation, there are *fewer* rather than more malpractice claims when lawyers unbundle services. Let me pose it to you this way: One client with a modest estate feels he cannot do it all alone and therefore needs legal representation. He is required to obtain and pay for legal services which he does not want and does not need because they are part of the "divorce package" and that is the only way to obtain the services that he most emphatically *does need*. He is understandably unhappy about paying for things he didn't want. The second client investigates his rights, decides which areas of his case he is comfortable taking responsibility for, negotiates a limited representation agreement with an attorney who does precisely what he has negotiated and no more. Which client do you think is most likely to be happy with the quality of the services rendered? And which one do you think is most likely to file a malpractice claim against his attorney?

Attorneys who have been routinely offering limited legal services find that their client satisfaction quotient jumps substantially. They do not get sued because the clients are happy. They got exactly what they wanted and bargained for and were not required by a rigid and unresponsive system to pay for what they neither want nor need.

User-friendly Attorneys

There is a growing number of attorneys who are not only willing, but pleased to offer limited legal services to family law clients. They are utterly disgusted with the rigidity of a system which assumes that everyone is too stupid to understand and contract for that which they need. They understand the need for limited legal services and derive satisfaction from the contribution they can make to reducing the conflict and pain in divorces.

Family law is one of the most difficult areas for attorneys, not only technically, but emotionally. Most are drawn to it because they genuinely want to help people. They have to be committed to it, because it is also one of the least lucrative areas of legal practice. Many of them have been utterly disillusioned and are now looking for ways to improve the system. Some received their training as mediators or as consulting attorneys to mediators, where litigants routinely take responsibility for their own divorces. Ask around and you will find attorneys willing to unbundle. A good place to start is with mediators and therapists. Appendix 4 contains a list of suggested questions.

5

How To Clarify Roles and Responsibilities

Clear Instructions

Rule Number One is to make no assumptions. Take the time to spell out *exactly* what you want the attorney to do and what you intend to do yourself. Fully discuss all of the legal and factual issues in your case. You will, in fact, spend *more* time with your attorney discussing the facts and legalities if you unbundle, because it is so critical that you are clear on what each of you is doing and how your roles intermesh. This is not a time to get cheap about paying your lawyer. The savings occur because you will only be paying for the services that you want and need.

The division of responsibility must be stated clearly and in writing. I don't mean to sound condescending, but you are a layman, not a lawyer, and there are lots of complications which you may not be aware of. Your lawyer will have to explain them to you. Don't make any assumptions without clarifying them with your attorney. Don't assume that an issue is simple because it seems to you as though it *should* be. Remember the quicksand issues; every state has them. Don't assume that your attorney is going to do something without confirming it specifically with him. Remember, we are talking about limiting legal services. That means, that the lawyer is only responsible for doing *what you specifically authorize and instruct him to do*. If you did not tell him you wanted discovery included on the list of his authorized activities, don't be surprised if subpoenas are not forthcoming. If you didn't tell him you wanted it, it is not going to happen. Clear communications and instructions will save lots of grief and later conversations about "but I thought that was part of what *you* were going to do . . . "

Put it in Writing

Again, leave no room for error. If you are going to do all of the discovery, say so. If you are going to go to the bank yourself and get copies of the bank records, but want the attorney to subpoena the other records, all of that has to be spelled out for the protection of both of you.

In Appendices 2, 3 and 4, I have provided a series of checklists and questions to ask your attorney in order to make sure that everyone understands their respective roles and responsibilities. Appendix 6 includes guidelines for retainer letters. Use these and update them as necessary.

Remember, your case is an organic evolving thing; as you obtain more information, the assumptions you made at the beginning may no longer be accurate. For example, if you felt discovery was going to be civil and informal, and preliminary investigation turns up a secret bank account or misappropriated funds, you may want to rethink the scope of representation you have agreed to. You may want discovery to be more formal and more thorough than originally planned.

All modifications to the agreement should also be in writing. You may find yourself saying to the attorney "I originally wanted you to just coach me on going to court, but I got handed my lunch last time, so now I want you to appear with me." If this is a change from the original instructions, write out your revised expectations, including changes in billing structures and payments, and make sure that you both sign it and keep a copy.

Keep the Attorney Informed

If he is going to have to periodically step in and out of your case, or only perform limited tasks and duties, it is critical that you keep him *fully* informed of everything that you do on your own. This includes any deals you make with the other side (substantive *or* procedural), facts you turn up (even if *you* don't think they are important). They may be critical in ways you could not possibly know.

He has to do the same with you. All this means that you will be paying a bit more than you otherwise would for your lawyer's time to chat and bring each other up to date on the status of what each of you has been doing. So be it. It will still cost much less than if you were paying for full service representation, and I expect that you will both be much more satisfied with your professional teamwork.

If you don't do this and decide to get cheap about the time you spend consulting with your attorney, you will be at a terrible disadvantage *vis a vis* other party. After all, he is in on all the conversations and discovery. The point here is to eliminate the services which you don't need, not to shoot yourself in the foot by eliminating the essential at the same time.

Finally, remember that the professional relationship and your needs may change over time. With the best intentions, you may find that you are in over your head and decide that for whatever reason, you need to turn it over to an attorney to handle for you. My friend Woody Mosten, who coined the term unbundling, uses the illustration of changing your own oil. Of course, with proper instruction and equipment, I expect we all could do it. However, after you have tried it a time or two, are you sure you want to?

6

A Word About Fairness

Most laymen blame attorneys for being overly litigious or promoting litigation. In some cases, they are right. However, most clients who sue their attorneys do so because they claim the attorney was not litigious enough. You have to make a choice here. If you want your case litigated to the hilt, unbundling is not for you.

If you are going to unbundle legal services, presumably your motivation is to streamline the process and reduce the cost by limiting the involvement of the lawyer. If you limit her involvement, you must also clearly limit her liability. It is not fair to tie her hands, then complain because the case is more complicated than you thought, or you did not get the result you wanted. Taking responsibility means *taking responsibility*. If you are not willing to do it, then go hire a shoot-em-up (bang, bang!) gunslinger and turn him loose on your spouse.

7

How to Screw Up
Your Case in
Five Easy Lessons

Most judges *loathe pro se* litigants. Sometimes this is legitimate. *Pro se* litigants make the judge's job harder because they usually don't know the rules or the legal culture. This means the case frequently takes more of their time than one with two knowledgeable lawyers involved. Also, *pro se* litigants are sometimes harder to control. After all, if a judge is getting mad and ready to throw the book at a lawyer, the lawyer may think about the next 15 cases that he is going to have before the same judge and bite his tongue a bit. The *pro se* litigant, who hopes he will never have to see this judge again, may go on blundering into a buzz saw without knowing any better.

The other reason judges hate *pro se* litigants, however, is that there are certain patterns which individuals who represent themselves tend to repeat over and over and over again, most of which make cases much more difficult.

If you really want to mess up your case, try one of the following:

Perry Mason Wannabes

Say you have always wished you had gone to law school. Perhaps you were a *Perry Mason* or *Divorce Court* junkie when you were a kid, and the real reason you want to limit legal services and represent yourself is so that you can play lawyer. *DON'T.* This isn't about giving rein to your ego or fantasy life. If you do, you are certain to be unsuccessful in court and embarrassed for making a fool of yourself.

Remember, you are a litigant who is representing himself. Don't try to be an attorney, or they will make mincemeat of you. Besides, after you have done it a few times, the joys of arguing in court are highly overrated.

Whine

Nothing will brand you more quickly as a difficult litigant and make the judge stop listening than if you want to use your day in court to cash in on all the "brown stamps" you have been collecting on your spouse through 15 years of marriage. If you are going to handle your own court appearances, find out in advance what is legally relevant and what is not, and limit yourself to the former. It may feel great to complain to an audience about the miserable failings of your spouse, but if you do, you will lose not only the audience but, most likely, your case.

Also, if you tick one judge off by your behavior, and then get transferred to another judge, don't assume there isn't carry over. The courthouse is a workplace much as any other. Once a case or litigant is labeled a "problem," that may well carry from court to court via the grapevine. You may well find the next judge even less sympathetic than the first.

One of the best uses you can make of your consulting attorney is as a sounding board, and let her coach you as to what is or is not useful for the judge to hear.

Also, do what the lawyers do. Watch the judge and look for signals. If the judge is losing patience with you or telling you to change the subject, *change the subject.* You will never score points with the judge by disregarding her instructions

Expect the Courts to Make Up for Your Inexperience

Some courts will loosen the rules a little for *pro se* litigants (to the disgust of opposing counsel, I might add). However, don't expect much. Judges are sworn to be even handed and fair to both sides. They *may* intervene if your opposing counsel is running you ragged with esoterica, but they won't (read: *can't*) do your work for you, and you should not expect it. Most of them will make a point of being absolutely impartial and won't cut you any slack whatsoever. Therefore, do your homework and expect that you will be held to the standard of any other litigant, represented or not.

Turn In Sloppy or Illegible Paperwork or Don't Serve Opposing Counsel With a Copy

This is guaranteed to make a judge nuts. I have already said that legal drafting is tricky. It needs to be clear and legible and the opposing side (whether represented or not) *must* be provided with a copy of whatever you file with the court. Rules vary from state to state and even county to county, but most of them require that documents be filed and served several days before any court appearance. Find out the rules, including the local variations, and adhere to them. Just because you are not a lawyer does not mean that a judge is not going to apply the rules and expect you to play by them. The worst of all possible results is that your paperwork is thrown out and you lose the case because you forgot to serve the other side or because it is so sloppy the judge can't read it.

This is particularly important when it comes to drafting orders. You have no idea how disastrous a badly-drafted order is when you later attempt to enforce it, and just because *you* think you know what it means doesn't guarantee that the judge will interpret it that way. It may also surprise you to learn that many experienced attorneys do lousy paperwork. Imagine how much harder it is to fill out the form properly if you have never seen it before.

Similarly, when a *pro se* litigant pulls out a shoebox full of receipts instead of properly prepared exhibits, any judge is going to inwardly groan. Be organized and do it right if you are going to do it at all.

Argue With the Judge

They *HATE* this. In some courts, it can get you held in contempt. Be courteous and professional. Plan on spending a lot of time hanging around the courthouse (without the kids, of course) if your case is being litigated. Educate yourself on the court procedures which apply to your case and, if possible, watch the judge who will be hearing it. You will learn a great deal about how he runs his courtroom and which arguments he responds to most favorably.

A particularly ineffective *pro se* trait is to raise your voice louder and louder as you repeat the arguments the judge has already rejected. Don't do it.

Finally, be realistic about what relief the court can and cannot grant. Many people are incredibly naive on this point and expect all sorts of things that the courts simply aren't equipped to deliver. Find out what is realistic and what is not and concentrate on the former. Above all, remember that if you are losing, you will never change the judge's opinion by arguing with him.

8

Attorney/Client Relations

The unbundling of services is new legal territory. This means that there is not a full set of ground rules which have been established as part of the time-honored tradition. Frankly, that isn't so bad. After all, isn't that what we are trying to get away from? There are, however, some common sense practices which will vastly improve the quality of your relationship with your limited services attorney, not to mention your ultimate satisfaction with the process.

Communicate Fully and Frequently

I have talked about this in depth before. Make sure that both of you are clear on what the other is and is not doing and that nothing slips through the cracks. Put all instructions in writing, as well as any modifications of the apportionment of your respective roles and responsibilities.

Make sure that you keep your attorney apprised of what is happening on your end of the case. This is for your own protection. The idea here is to make the process work for you. You don't want your attorney to find himself at a disadvantage, simply because you didn't get around to sharing important information with him (or were trying to save a buck).

Ask Questions

Don't hesitate to ask if you don't understand something. Remember, this isn't about ego, but rather taking responsibility for your process. If you are in it for the ego strokes, you will get creamed. It is better to admit if you don't know something and educate yourself on it than to leave a part of your body (or your financial future) on the courtroom floor because you did not want to spend the money to find out if your assumptions were correct. If you are going to effectively represent yourself, even in only part of your case, you are going to have to educate yourself about what that means, including the applicable law, procedures, benefits and risks. The only way to do this is to ask.

Pay Your Attorney as You Go

Most attorneys will insist on this if they are offering limited legal services. Remember, the reason you are doing this is presumably to limit your expense. It will not help you to build up a huge bill in consulting services. You are buying time and information from your attorney. That is his stock in trade as much as car repair services are to a mechanic. You want him to be responsive when you call from the courthouse and need his immediate opinion on an offer you have just received in a settlement conference. If you haven't been paying him, his office rent is due, and he's got another call from someone who pays like clockwork on the other line, who do you think is going to get his immediate attention? Think about it. Mediators are generally paid on the spot for services rendered, and most unbundled attorneys will expect it as well.

Ending the Relationship

This can be easy if your attorney is simply functioning as the consulting attorney or coach, answering your questions as you call: if you don't call, your relationship ends.

On the other hand, if you decided to unbundle horizontally, you will need to give clear instructions to terminate actions which are not done on an "as requested" basis, such as ongoing discovery, motions, court appearances, etc. If you don't want him to continue, it is *your* responsibility to make that clear, and in writing.

If, after trying it for a while, you decide that unbundling just isn't working and you need a full service lawyer, renegotiate the retainer letter. Remember, you carefully negotiated a limited services engagement. If that changes and you want standard full service, insist that the letter be revised and re-executed to reflect that change in your respective roles and responsibilities.

9

Epilogue

If, after going through the process described in the previous chapters and the appendices, you have decided that you are a good candidate for limited legal services, congratulations. You have stepped into the forefront of legal reform and taken responsibility for your own life.

There are two ways that the legal culture changes. One is for legislatures to pass new and different laws. We have already seen where that has gotten us.[1]

The second is a grassroots movement where people who find that the existing institution does not work voluntarily take themselves out of it and devise a better way to solve their problem. That is precisely what unbundling does. Very few state bar organizations or legislatures have endorsed it. Nevertheless, family law litigants and progressive family lawyers all over the country are doing it anyway. Ironically, of course, if enough people do it and build a track record demonstrating a better way of solving legal problems, the very success of the grassroots system will generate its own political correctness. Legislators will then be only too happy to jump on the bandwagon, give the now-proven system official recognition, and probably take credit for its success. So be it. I don't give a rip who gets the credit. What I care about is replacing what does not work with something that does.

---

[1]This is not to say that future legislatures may not be wiser than past ones, but political correctness, special interest groups and the fear of losing the re-election bid being what they are, it would be best if we don't hold our breath.

As you work with the concepts outlined in this guide, they will evolve. The ideas are new, and this book is not intended to be the final word. The techniques are changing by trial and error, and as litigants and attorneys experiment with different ways to do it, they will create approaches and solutions that I have not thought of. That is the beauty of being in on something new and being willing to experiment. We can find out what works and what doesn't.

As long as we behave as helpless victims of a system out of control, that is precisely what we will be. If instead we take responsibility for making it work for families, we can have all of the joy of knowing that we have taken back the power over our lives, for ourselves and our children. I assure you that if we do, they will bless us.

Appendices

Issues Presented by My Case

Before you can decide whether you are a good candidate for limited legal services, you must understand the issues presented by your case. Only then can you properly evaluate the risks of limiting legal services and the possible consequences of taking on some of the responsibility for your own representation.

The following is a *partial* list. Divorces are as individual as the couples involved, and there are frequently hidden problems or complications which your consulting attorney will spot. Be sure you ask her to point them out to you so you can make informed decisions. Among the issues which you will need to consider are the following:

Issues Involving Children:

Is there a dispute about custody of your children? Visitation or timeshare? Where they go to school? To church?

Is the disagreement likely to be resolved by mediation?

Is a formal custody evaluation likely to be required?

Is it likely that you will have a contested trial?

What kinds of witnesses or evidence are likely to be presented by your side? By your spouse's?

Does one of you want to take the kids and move away?

Are there contentions that one of you is an unfit parent?

Are there allegations of physical violence or substance abuse in the family?

Issues Involving Support:

Is the income of both of you easily ascertained (as in a W-2, paystub or some other available document)?

How likely is it that there is additional income from other sources which must be discovered or evaluated?

How difficult is it going to be to get the information necessary to prove the additional income?

Will you need to subpoena records or take depositions?

Is it likely that an outside party will have to go over records to find missing income? Should this be an attorney? A paralegal? An accountant?

Is alimony going to be in dispute? If you agree it will be paid, do you agree on the amount? Do you agree on the duration?

Is there a computer support guideline in effect in your state? Who is going to run it for you? Do you have all the information necessary to obtain a correct figure? If not, do you know how you are going to get it?

Are there subjective support issues which need to be addressed or developed, such as marital standard of living? What information is required to prove it? What is the best way to assemble the it?

Issues Involving Property:

Does your state make a distinction between separate and joint property?

Is that likely to make a difference in the property division in your case?

What kinds of evidence need to be developed to decide it?

What kinds of property do you have to divide?

> Real property (land and buildings)

> Personal property (furniture and appliances, etc.)

> Employee benefits (pensions, 401(k) plans, IRA accounts and the like)

> Stocks and bonds (including stock options)

> Business interests

> Other types of property recognized as divisible by your state law.

What special problems are presented by each type of property?

Was any of your property inherited? What complications does that present?

As to each of these kinds of property, what witnesses or documentary evidence will be required to present your case, and what is the best way to develop it?

Do you suspect your spouse of hiding assets? How do you propose to find them?

Other Issues:

Is there a history of domestic violence? What complications does that present to your representing yourself in part?

Does the date of separation make a difference in property division in your state, and is it in dispute?

Is there a premarital agreement which impacts the division of property? Support rights?

Is there inherited money which has been invested in any part of your marital estate?

What other complications are presented by the facts of your case? [*Always* ask this question of your consulting attorney or coach.]

Checklist for Limited Legal Services

The following is a partial list of duties and responsibilities which might be apportioned between you and your attorney. It is *not exhaustive*, for the simple reason that each state and each individual case is different, and if it were complete enough to cover all contingencies, it would be virtually meaningless to most of you. Therefore, it is intended to suggest areas which you should explore with your attorney.

When discussing your respective responsibilities with your attorney, it would be useful to make a notation as to who is going to take responsibility for each function. Don't forget, however, that your case may well require evidence and services which are not listed here. Discuss this with your attorney.

This list can then be used as *the basis for* a written retainer agreement. NOTE: IT IS NOT A SUBSTITUTE FOR A WRITTEN RETAINER AGREEMENT.

Information Gathering:

Who will obtain the financial data (bank records, registers, pension statements, real estate documents)?

Who will obtain the information regarding custody and visitation disputes?

Income and expense data?

Formal Discovery:

Do we need formal discovery?

Who will subpoena records?

Who will prepare requests for documents and evaluate the results?

Who will prepare and evaluate Interrogatories?

Are depositions required? Who will take them?

Draft Documents:

Who will prepare the court forms?

Motions and responses?

Affidavits and declarations?

Who will see that they are properly filed and served?

Analyze paperwork filed by the other side?

Who will prepare Orders?

Other court documents as may be necessary?

Legal Research:

Who will be responsible for researching the applicable law?

Will this include writing briefs and memoranda?

Advise Clients:

Who will advise you on the relevant law?

Procedures?

Strategy and tactics?

Negotiations:

Who is responsible for negotiating with the other side?

How will you be sure you exchange the information you have both obtained for maximum efficiency and effectiveness?

Court Appearances:

Who will appear at hearings?

Settlement conferences?

Trials?

Appeals?

If you are doing any of this yourself, will your attorney prep you?

Is there any ethical prohibition of scripting or ghostwriting in your state?

Other Services:

What other services will your attorney or coach provide you?

Use of a client library?

Direction to resources to check at the law library?

Forms?

Strategy and Tactics:

Who is responsible for setting the strategy of the case?

If you are each doing part of it, how will you be sure you are coordinating sufficiently so that each of you is fully informed of everything you need to know to perform your part of the deal effectively?

Tasks to be Apportioned

As with the other Appendices, this is intended to be a guide only. Your state or local court may have different rules, and other tasks may need to be assigned between you and your attorney.

If something is to be done by a paralegal rather than an attorney, note that on the form. Then, *make this the basis of a formal retainer or engagement letter. THIS CHECKLIST IS NOT SUFFICIENT TO FULLY DESCRIBE ALL THE RIGHTS AND DUTIES YOU AND YOUR ATTORNEY NEED TO ADDRESS.*

Task	Attorney to Do:	I Will Do:
Draft papers to start divorce		
File and serve papers		
Draft Motions		
Draft affidavits and declarations		
Analyze case and advise of legal rights		
Procedural advice		
Formulate strategy and tactics		
Investigate facts		
Obtain documents		
Draft correspondence		
Review correspondence and pleadings		
Appear in court		
Run computer support programs		
Subpoena documents		
Take depositions		
Review depositions and documents obtained from other sources		
Legal research and analysis		
Contact witnesses		
Draft or analyze settlement proposals		
Select expert witnesses		
Draft orders and judgments		
Outline testimony		
Trial or negotiation preparation		
Review orders and judgments drafted by client		
Review other documents to be drafted by client		
Enforce orders		
Draft other papers as necessary		

Unbundling Horizontally

These issues will be handled start to finish by:

Issue	Attorney	Client
Custody or visitation disputes		
Child support and alimony		
Real property division		
Personal property division[1]		
Business interests		
Bank accounts		
Investments		
Pension rights[2]		
Stocks and bonds		
Employee benefits		
Health insurance		
Life Insurance		
Other issues:		

---

[1] This means furniture and pots and pans, folks. Unless it is worth a fortune, think twice before you pay someone to do this for you. For other options, see my earlier book *How to Avoid the Divorce from Hell*, chapter 38, "Reasonable Solutions to Problems That Come Up In Every Divorce."

[2] This is extremely technical. Most attorneys farm this out to specialists because it is so easy to screw up. I've never seen a *pro se* who can get a Qualified Domestic Relations Order ("QDRO," pronounced "quadro") right and the consequences of doing it wrong are horrendous.

Questions to Ask Your Lawyer[1]

What is your experience with limited legal services?

What are your requirements for apportioning our respective responsibilities regarding my case?

Will you work as my coach, advising me on law, procedure or tactics from time to time as I request it?

Will you perform designated services such as research, drafting or discovery, while I assume responsibility for other areas of the case?

Are you willing to handle an entire issue such as custody or support from start to finish while I assume responsibility for the remaining issues?

What is your experience with cases such as mine? Have you handled similar cases in the traditional way? Unbundled?

If I want to represent myself in depositions or court appearances, will you coach me?

Will you outline questions for testimony if I request it?

---

[1]These questions are tailored to unbundling only. If you are considering full service representation, see the detailed discussion in my book *How to Avoid the Divorce from Hell*, Chapter 7.

If I want to negotiate my own settlement, will you coach me?

Will you draft declarations and affidavits for me? Orders?

Do you have a client library? Do you charge for its use?

What are the pitfalls I should be aware of if I decide to do part of the case myself? Will you coach me on how to avoid them?

Will you prepare a written retainer letter reflecting our agreements apportioning the responsibility of the case between us?

What are your billing rates and expectations of payment?

What issues do you see in my case which are particularly troublesome? What is your recommendation for the best way to approach them?

Questions to Ask a Paralegal

There is a much greater variation in the depth and quality of the training and experience of family law paralegals than family law attorneys. This is because there is no standardized training system for paralegals. Some go through rigorous programs to obtain degrees; other programs do little more than teach them the basics of many different fields. This means that they may or may not have in depth family law training, even if they have a degree from a paralegal program.

Many paralegals who work in family law firms are not authorized to do more than fill out forms. Others have developed significant specialties in areas such as the division of pensions and complex family law discovery.

The best test of a paralegal's ability to help you effectively is long-term experience doing *exactly* what you need them to do for other clients. Many of them have spent years in family law firms before deciding to free lance, and these are likely to have the most thorough grounding in the areas you will need. The only way to find out is to *ask*. But don't assume that a paralegal degree alone qualifies them to do what you need. Also, remember that they are not qualified to give you legal advice because they are not trained to do so. The rules on this vary widely from state to state. Find out the rules in your state.

Among the questions you should ask are the following:

What is the nature of your paralegal training? Where did you obtain it? How long have you been doing this kind of work? Where?

What is your experience with cases such as mine?

Are you familiar with the court rules and procedures which apply to my case?

Are you experienced in drafting court forms similar to the ones I will need? Declarations? Orders?

What is your experience with discovery? Are you used to drafting interrogatories? Subpoenas? Deposition notices? [In big firms, paralegals may do virtually all of this; in small firms, they may or may not.]

What experience do you have in analyzing financial data? Tracing? Accounting? [I had a paralegal who was great at this, but most aren't; ask the question if it is relevant to your case preparation.]

What experience do you have in preparing exhibits for trial? Are you familiar with the rules in my jurisdiction for the format and time deadlines for court exhibits? [If they worked in a big firm, they may have had primary responsibility for discovery and exhibits; find this out.]

What is your experience in preparing Qualified Domestic Relations Orders for pension benefits? [Many paralegals have developed a specialty in this area, depending on where they worked before deciding to go into business for themselves.]

What are your billing requirements and rates?

Do you carry malpractice insurance?

Guidelines for Retainer Letters

A retainer letter is the written record of the agreement between an attorney and a client. Other terms meaning the same thing are engagement letter or fee agreement. The requirements of such letters are frequently fixed by state law or State Bar ethics opinions, and vary widely from state to state. Most states require some form of written agreement for any but the most casual contact.

If you are to successfully unbundle legal services, it is essential that you and your attorney sign an agreement which clearly defines the tasks to be performed by each of you.

It would be impossible to draft a single agreement which would meet the needs of all states and all situations. Therefore, these suggestions are intended to be guidelines for the terms to be included in the final agreement, not definitive in themselves.

A limited services agreement should include the following, *at a minimum*:

Who is going to go "of record" (that is, put their name on the papers filed with the court).

Who is going to prepare, file and serve legal paperwork (including motions, affidavits, and any other documents required to be filed) and be responsible for compliance with court rules and deadlines.

Who is responsible for setting strategy.

Who is responsible for gathering information including apportioning discovery tasks.

Who will make court appearances.

Who will draft correspondence.

Who is responsible for negotiating with the opposing side.

Whether tasks are being divided on a subject by subject basis.

If so, who is handling which subject areas, and what happens if they overlap.

Whether the fees are hourly (and if so, what is included) or by some other measure.

If not hourly, the method for determining them (i.e. flat fee or task by task).

Whether a deposit or retainer is required and whether it is held in trust until earned.

That *all modifications will be in writing and signed by both parties.*

The foregoing are minimum terms which should be spelled out. Your state may require additional "standard" terms, and your case may include special agreements not detailed her. Make sure it is complete and accurate before you sign it.

Self Test

BE HONEST. Do the following self-test *in writing*. Don't just read it and answer it mentally. You won't be as thorough in your analysis if you don't force yourself to put pen to paper. You also won't be as effective in revising it as needed if you don't have a written record to refer to.

Goals For Limiting Legal Services:

What are my goals in my divorce? [See Appendix 8 for more information on this.]

Why do I want to limit legal services?

   Save money

   Retain more control over the process?

   Why?

Retain more control over my spouse?[Lose 5 points if your answer is yes]

Other reasons? List all perceived advantages.

What risks do I see if I represent myself in whole or in part? List all perceived disadvantages.

My Strengths and Weaknesses

What am I good at? [Be brutally honest here.]

Paperwork

Writing

Public speaking

Computers

Investigation and information gathering

Research

Analysis of documents

Financial planning and analysis

Decision making

Am I disciplined in my work? Organized?

Other skills I have which will assist me:

Attention to detail

Persistence

Follow through

Can I consistently meet deadlines?

Can I understand and use support guidelines?

Do computers intimidate me?

Which of the above do I really hate doing [Be *brutally* honest here; if you really hate doing something, you won't like it better if it is part of your divorce. Instead, you'll hate it more and do a lousy job.]

If I'm not good at it, can I find someone else who is and hire them to do that part?

Which tasks would be better delegated to someone with greater expertise?

If I'm not good at it, can I find someone else to teach me how to do it, supervise or check my work?

Who?

Which specific tasks am I going to delegate or seek help with? Write them here, and write the name or designation of the person who will help you next to each one (i.e., paralegal, attorney, etc.)

Time Commitment:

Do I have the time to do it properly?

Will my other responsibilities suffer?

Is there a way to compensate for it by delegating some of my other responsibilities for work, etc.

Emotional Consequences:

Can I handle it emotionally?

Am I motivated by a desire to keep up the fight?

Am I able to stand firm and not give up too much simply to have it over with?

Am I trying to get even for things my spouse did to me?

Can I separate my emotions from decisions involving money and property?

Can I separate money and property from decisions involving the kids?

Am I willing to find a trusted independent person (attorney, paralegal or friend) who is disinterested and who will be brutally frank with me if I allow one issue to spill over into another?

Will I commit to listen to them if they tell me I am off track? Even if they tell me what I *really* don't want to hear?

Am I willing to do a cost-benefit analysis at every stage to be
sure I'm devoting my time, energy and money where they
will do the most good?

Do I really want resolution, or am I trying to remain engaged
with my spouse?

Am I afraid of confrontation with my spouse? With others?

Is there a history of physical or verbal abuse in my marriage?

Has my spouse threatened me if I seek legal help? [Many do.]

Is that impacting my decision to limit legal services?

Is it in my best interests to have a third person act as a buffer
between my spouse and myself?

The Kids:

Will my children suffer if I represent myself?

Will my attention be diverted from them?

Will it take time away from them?

If I am working on this at home, can I be sure they don't see or hear what is going on?

Can I keep them absolutely out of the case, as I recognize it is my obligation to do?

Will I commit to keep all written materials out of their reach and under lock and key?

Will I commit not to discuss the divorce in front of them, either on the phone or with others in their presence?

Will I commit to make arrangements for someone to care for them when I have to go to court (even just to file papers) so they will not be exposed to it?

Responsibility:

How much responsibility am I willing to take?

Am I willing to take complete responsibility for the outcome?

If no, which areas am I willing to be responsible for?

Am I willing to take the time to educate myself fully on my legal rights and responsibilities?

Am I comfortable making decisions and sticking to them?

Am I willing to take the risk of being wrong?

Am I willing to accept the likelihood that I won't know things that the attorney on the other side does, and that lack of knowledge may place me at a disadvantage?

Do I believe the advantages of partial self-representation outweigh the disadvantages?

What are they? List them here:

If it turns out that I misjudged and don't get what I thought I should have, am I willing know that I made the best decision under the circumstances and to live with the consequences?

My Goals for This Divorce

Find at least one hour when you will be uninterrupted, and write out your goals for your divorce. Make sure to ask your consulting attorney or coach if your legal and financial goals are realistic, and if not, why not. Answer them fully on a separate sheet of paper.

What kind of relationship do I want with my kids when this is over?

What kind of relationship do I want with my ex when this is over?

Where do I expect to live?

What kind of work will I do?

What kind of income do I expect to have? From what sources?

Will I be able to live comfortably on it?

What investments do I expect to have?

What kind of house do I expect to live in?

What property will I have after it is divided and the costs of the proceeding are paid?

How much responsibility am I willing to assume for all of this?

When I look in a mirror five years from now, what do I want to be able to say to myself about the way I handled my divorce?

Index

M. Sue Talia

$\mathbf{M}$. Sue Talia brings a wealth of experience in the area of family law and is recognized as one of the foremost family lawyers in the East Bay. For the past twenty years, her law practice has focused on complex family law litigation, from custody to cases of first impression in the state of California, including some of the largest estates ever addressed by the family law courts in this area.

She is a founding director and former president of the Family Law Section of the Contra Costa Bar Association, one of the most progressive family law groups in the nation. In conjunction with that organization, she has been actively involved in family law legal reform, writing extensively and testifying at legislative hearings on family law issues.

An experienced public speaker, she has addressed numerous civic and professional groups on family law issues, and has been invited back repeatedly to the same groups. She has taught numerous workshops both to litigants and attorneys on family law matters. These range from a basic 8 hour course in what the family law courts can (and cannot) do, to courses on Marital Standard of Living, Preparing and Litigating the High Income Support Case, and other programs geared to educating lawyers and judges. She has also been a repeat speaker at the California Society of CPA's semi-annual symposium on Family Law, receiving high marks as a speaker and lecturer.

She brings sensitivity and humor to her discussions, which are always geared toward practical solutions to problems rather than esoteric legal theory. She is a master at demystifying the system, exposing both its strengths and weaknesses to her listeners and readers.

Since 1977, she has limited her practice to family law, first in Danville, and now in San Ramon, California. Formerly known as M. Sue Greicar, she now limits her practice to allow more time for her writing and legal reform activities. A key component of those at present is her support of the consumer-based "unbundling" movement in California, which promotes limited legal services to streamline and demythologize the family law system.

She graduated from the University of Santa Clara *summa cum laude* in 1971, obtained a Master's degree in American History from Stanford University in 1974 and a J.D. degree from Hastings College of the Law in 1977.

She is the author of *How to Avoid the Divorce from Hell (and dance together at your daughter's wedding)* published by Nexus Publishing Company in 1996.

Did you borrow this book?

Want a copy of your own?

Please send _______ copies of *A Client's Guide to Limited Legal Services* at $10.95 per copy.

Please send _______ copies of *How to Avoid the Divorce from Hell (and Dance Together at Your Daughter's Wedding)* at $12.95 per copy.

Please add $3.00 per book for postage and handling. California residents add applicable sales tax. Allow 30 days for delivery.

Send check payable to Nexus Publishing Company to 480 San Ramon Valley Boulevard, Suite A, Danville, CA 94526.

Call credit card orders to 1-800-393-0751 or fax to (510) 743-1614.

Name ____

Phone (________) _______________________________

Address____

City _______________________ State________ Zip____________

Enclosed is my check/money order for $__________________

Bill my   VISA________   MasterCard__________

Account No. ______________________________ Expires ___________

Signature ____

Quantity Orders Invited

Did you borrow this book? Want a copy of your own?

Please send _______ copies of *A Client's Guide to Limited Legal Services* at $10.95 per copy. Please send _______ copies of *How to Avoid the Divorce from Hell (and Dance Together at Your Daughter's Wedding)* at $12.95 per copy.

Please add $3.00 per book for postage and handling. California residents include applicable sales tax. Allow 30 days for delivery. Send check payable to Nexus Publishing Company to 480 San Ramon Valley Boulevard, Suite A, Danville, CA 94526.

Call credit card orders to 1-800-393-0751 or fax to (510) 743-1614.

Name ________________________________ Phone (__________) ________________

Address ____

City ____________________________ State __________ Zip__________________

Enclosed is my check/money order for $ ____________________

Bill my   VISA__________   MasterCard __________

Account No. ________________________________ Expires __________________

Signature ____

Did you borrow this book? Want a copy of your own?

Please send _______ copies of *A Client's Guide to Limited Legal Services* at $10.95 per copy. Please send _______ copies of *How to Avoid the Divorce from Hell (and Dance Together at Your Daughter's Wedding)* at $12.95 per copy.

Please add $3.00 per book for postage and handling. California residents include applicable sales tax. Allow 30 days for delivery. Send check payable to Nexus Publishing Company to 480 San Ramon Valley Boulevard, Suite A, Danville, CA 94526.

Call credit card orders to 1-800-393-0751 or fax to (510) 743-1614.

Name ________________________________ Phone (__________) ________________

Address ____

City ____________________________ State __________ Zip__________________

Enclosed is my check/money order for $ ____________________

Bill my   VISA__________   MasterCard __________

Account No. ________________________________ Expires __________________

Signature ____

From: _____________________

____

____

____

Place
Stamp
Here

Nexus Publishing Company
480 San Ramon Valley Boulevard, Suite A
Danville, CA 94526

From: _____________________

____

____

____

Place
Stamp
Here

Nexus Publishing Company
480 San Ramon Valley Boulevard, Suite A
Danville, CA 94526